What Are Budgets?

Working with Decimals

Andrew Einspruch

Publishing Credits

Editor
Sara Johnson

Editorial Director
Emily R. Smith, M.A.Ed.

Editor-in-Chief
Sharon Coan, M.S.Ed.

Creative Director
Lee Aucoin

Publisher
Rachelle Cracchiolo, M.S.Ed.

Image Credits

Teacher Created Materials

5301 Oceanus Drive
Huntington Beach, CA 92649-1030
http://www.tcmpub.com

ISBN 978-0-7439-0877-1
© 2008 Teacher Created Materials, Inc.
Reprinted 2012

Table of Contents

What Is a Budget? 4

Budgets Are Everywhere. 8

A Simple Budget. 10

Your Own Budget 12

Stick to It! 20

Sam's Savings 21

Changes in Budget 23

Keep Going 26

Problem-Solving Activity 28

Glossary 30

Index 31

Answer Key 32

What Is a Budget?

A budget is a plan for money. It has 2 parts: **income** and **expenses** (ex-PEN-suhz). Income is money that someone gets. You might get an **allowance**. Expenses are things that money is spent on, like food or clothes.

Buying food at the supermarket

Some children receive an allowance.

"Bag" Your Budget!

The word *budget* comes from an old French word for bag, or purse. A *bouge* (BOOJ) was a leather bag used to carry money.

A budget helps you make sure you do not spend more than you can **afford**. It helps you plan your income (money you will get) and expenses (money you will spend).

Some children earn incomes by doing paper routes.

LET'S EXPLORE MATH

Spending Money Place Value

Would you rather have $12.00 spending money or $21.00 spending money? Like most people, you probably would like $21.00 spending money! That's because it's a larger amount.

The **value** of each number in the spending money depends on its place, or **position** (puh-ZIH-shuhn), in that number.

Tens	Ones
1	2
2	1

a. In $12.00, what is the dollar value of 1?

b. In $21.00, what is the dollar value of 1?

c. In $21.00, what is the dollar value of 2?

Making Good Choices

Budgets can help you make the most of your money. They are a good way of helping you think better and make better choices.

Often, money is written in **decimal** (DES-uh-muhl) form. A decimal point separates the dollars and the cents. Dollars are whole numbers and are to the left of a decimal point. Cents are shown to the right of a decimal point.

There are 100 cents in a dollar. The numbers to the right of the decimal point show the part (or fraction) of 100 cents, or part of 1 dollar. The 2 place values after the decimal point are the tenths and hundredths places.

So, $1.05 = 1 dollar and 05 cents or 1 and 5 hundredths of a dollar. $2.85 = 2 dollars and 85 cents or 2 and 85 hundredths of a dollar.

$1.05 and $2.85 are shown like this in the table below:

Tens	Ones	Decimal Point	Tenths	Hundredths
	1	.	0	5
	2	.	8	5

Draw the table above. Then show:

a. $1.20   **b.** $15.50   **c.** $21.05

Let's say you wanted to buy a new bike. A budget would help you plan how much you would need to save and for how long.

Budgets and Time

A budget is a plan that covers a length of time. It can be for any amount of time—a week, a month, or even a year.

Budgets Are Everywhere

Who uses budgets? Families and **individuals** (in-duh-VIH-juh-wuhls) use them. So do businesses, **charities**, and **governments**. In fact, anyone who needs to plan income and expenses uses a budget.

Budgets can be for small amounts, like someone's allowance and expenses. They can also be for trillions of dollars, like the budget for a nation's government.

Each year, the United States government releases a budget for the nation.

Millions, Billions, and Trillions

How much is 1 million? What does 1 billion look like? Is there really such a thing as a trillion?

Well, yes, there is. But it is such an enormous number that it can really be difficult to understand. Let's start with 1 million.

1 million is 1,000 × 1,000.
It looks like this: 1,000,000.

1 billion is 1,000 × 1 million.
It looks like this: 1,000,000,000.

1 trillion is 1,000 × 1 billion.
It looks like this: 1,000,000,000,000.

A Simple Budget

Let's look at a simple budget. Sam gets $5.00 per week allowance. She also earns $15.50 per week helping her neighbor, Ms. Liu, in the garden. Both amounts are her income.

LET'S EXPLORE MATH

Sam earns $15.50 per week from Ms. Liu. This is how Ms. Liu paid her: 1 × $10.00 bill; 5 × $1.00 bills; 4 dimes, and 10 pennies.

a. Did Ms. Liu give Sam the right amount of money?

b. Draw the table below and show how much money Sam earns in a week from her allowance and gardening.

Tens	Ones	Decimal Point	Tenths	Hundredths
		.		

Sam's expenses include $9.50 per week on a movie ticket and $5.00 per week on eating out. At the end of each week, Sam has $6.00 left after her expenses. She puts this $6.00 in her savings.

Sam's Weekly Budget

Income

Allowance	$5.00
Money from Ms. Liu	$15.50
Total income	**$20.50**

Expenses

Movies	$9.50
Eating out	$5.00
Total expenses	**$14.50**

Total income – total expenses = savings

$20.50 – $14.50 = $6.00

Your Own Budget

So, how do you make a budget? The first step is to keep track of your income and expenses—just like Sam did.

Start by writing down what you earn and spend in a notebook. Do this for a few weeks. This helps you keep track of your money each week.

My Budget

Week 1

Earned

Allowance	$7.25
Paper route	$20.00

Spent

Pizza	$5.25
Movie	$9.75
Comic book	$2.00
Swimming	$4.00
Trading cards	$2.25

Week 2

Earned

Allowance	$7.25
Paper route	$20.00

Spent

Comic book	$2.00
Movie	$9.75
Sandwich	$5.25
Trading cards	$2.25
Swimming	$4.00

Plan Ahead

Next, you need to plan ahead. What do you need to save for? Once you know, you can plan for the weeks ahead. Under the heading *Income*, make a list of what you will earn. This might include your allowance or money from extra chores at home.

My Weekly Budget

Income

Allowance	$7.25
Money from paper route	$20.00
Extra chores at home	$5.50

LET'S EXPLORE MATH

Use the income list above to answer the questions.

a. Write the income items in order from the greatest amount to the least amount.

b. What is the total weekly income? *Hint*: When you add decimals, always line up the decimal points one under the other.

Now, make a list under the heading *Expenses*. Write down what you think you will spend money on. This might include food, movies, CDs—it's up to you! The information in your notebook will help you work it all out.

My Weekly Budget

Expenses

Eating out	$5.25
Entertainment	$4.00
Movies	$9.75
Comic books	$4.00

Budget Categories

Use **categories** (KAT-uh-gore-eez) to group things together in your budget. It helps you to keep track of everything. For example, movies, concerts, and DVDs might all go into one category called *Entertainment*. A category called *Eating out* might include any food you buy, like pizza or sandwiches.

How Much Is Left Over?

Now, add up all the things in your *Income* list. This will be your total income. Then add up all the things in your *Expenses* list to get your total expenses.

Next, subtract the total expenses from the total income. This will tell you how much money you'll have left at the end of the week. This money can go in your savings.

My Weekly Budget

Income

Allowance	$7.25
Money from paper route	$20.00
Extra chores at home	$5.50
Total income	**$32.75**

Expenses

Eating out	$5.25
Entertainment	$4.00
Movies	$9.75
Comic books	$4.00
Total expenses	$23.00

Total income − total expenses = $9.75 savings

LET'S EXPLORE MATH

Carlos has been saving to buy a computer game. The game costs $22.50. Carlos empties his piggy bank and counts how much money he has saved so far.

a. In his piggy bank, Carlos has 2 × $5.00 bills, 4 × quarters, and 10 × dimes. How much money does he have?

b. How much more money does Carlos need to save? *Hint:* When you subtract decimals, always line up the decimal points with each other.

Stick to It!

Well done! You have made your first budget. But it is not enough to just make a list of what you might spend. If you want your budget to work, you have to stick to it.

Budgeting Tip: Using Computers to Help You Budget

A computer is a great tool for budgeting. It is really just a fancy version of your notebook. It allows you to make a list of income and expense categories. It allows you to make changes. And sometimes it does the math for you!

Sam's Savings

Sam wants to save for a DVD. The DVD will cost $30.00. She knows from her budget that she has $6.00 left at the end of each week. But Sam does not want to change her expenses. She really enjoys going to the movies and eating out.

Sam needed to figure out how long it would take to save $30.00. So she has worked out that it will take her 5 weeks to save for the DVD. It will be a long 5 weeks, but it will be worth it!

cost of DVD ÷ savings per week = number of weeks
$30.00   ÷ $6.00   =   5 weeks

LET'S EXPLORE MATH

After 5 weeks, Sam had finally saved enough money to buy the DVD. At the store, she gets a surprise. The DVD is on sale!

a. Sam buys the DVD and receives $5.50 change. How much was the DVD?

b. With her change, Sam buys some candy. It costs 75¢. How much money does she have left now?

Changes in Budget

What if something happens to change your income or your expenses? You have to make sure that you change your budget, too.

Update Your Budget

Remember that a budget is a plan. Plans need to be updated as things change. If you earn less money or have an unexpected expense, change your budget. Try to reduce your expenses.

Let's look at Sam's budget again. What if something happened that changed her budget? Sam earns $5.00 per week allowance. She earns $15.50 per week from Ms. Liu. Her expenses are $9.50 per week on movies and $5.00 per week for eating out.

But what if Ms. Liu went on vacation for a week, and she did not need Sam to help her? That would mean a pretty big change to Sam's budget!

Sam's (Revised) Weekly Budget

Income

Allowance:	$5.00
Total income:	$5.00

Expenses

Eating out:	$5.00
Total expenses:	$5.00

Sam can't go to the movies the week that Ms. Liu is on vacation. She can still eat out, but she won't have money left for her savings. So it will take her an extra week to save for her DVD.

LET'S EXPLORE MATH

Sam's friend Nisha is sick and she has asked Sam to do her paper route for 2 days. How much extra money will Sam earn in 2 days if she gets $3.50 each day?

Keep Going

Budgets can be very **detailed** or very simple. But no matter how big or how small, every budget is really the same. It's a plan that maps out everything that is earned and everything that is spent.

So, now that you've started to keep a budget, keep going. It might just help you to make sure that you can afford to do all the things that you want to do!

Hot Dog Heaven

Chris plays on a local basketball team. The team needs new uniforms, but the club does not have any money. New uniforms cost $5.00 each. Chris wants to help in any way he can. He has decided to raise some money by setting up a hot dog stand at his school fair. He wants to sell 100 hot dogs. He works out the cost of the ingredients. These are his expenses.

50 hot dogs = $100.00

50 hot dog buns = $25.00

4 bottles of ketchup = $14.00

4 jars of mustard = $16.00

Solve It!

a. If Chris sells all 100 hot dogs for $3.50 each, how much money will he earn? This is his income.

b. How much money did Chris make after paying for his expenses? This is his profit.

c. How many uniforms will the club be able to buy?

Use the steps below to help you solve the problems.

Step 1: Find the cost of 100 hot dogs, 100 hot dog buns, 8 bottles of ketchup, and 8 jars of mustard.
Hint: Double the costs listed on page 28.

Step 2: Add up all the expenses.

Step 3: Find the income from the sale of 100 hot dogs.

Step 4: Subtract the cost of expenses from the income from the sales. The money left over is the profit. Chris can use the profit to buy the uniforms.

Step 5: Divide the profit by $5.00.

Glossary

afford—to be able to pay for something

allowance—a fixed amount of pocket money

categories—groups within a system; budgets can have different categories

charities—organizations that give to people in need

decimal—a number based on 10

detailed—having lots of parts shown

expenses—things that people spend money on

governments—groups of leaders usually chosen by the people of a certain area to manage that area

income—an amount of money earned

individuals—single people, not people in a group

position—the order, or place, of something

value—the amount of something

Index

allowance, 4, 9, 10–11, 13, 14–15, 19, 24

decimals, 6, 10, 15, 19

expenses, 4–5, 8–9, 11, 12, 16, 18–19, 20, 21, 23–24, 29

governments, 8–9

income, 4–5, 8, 10–11, 12, 14–15, 18–19, 20, 23–24, 28–29

money, 4–6, 10, 12, 14, 16, 18–19, 22, 23, 25, 28, 29

profit, 29

savings, 7, 11, 14, 18–19, 21–22, 25

Let's Explore Math

Page 5:
a. The value of 1 is $10.00
b. The value of 1 is $1.00
c. The value of 2 is $20.00

Page 6:

Tens	Ones	Decimal Point	Tenths	Hundredths
	1	.	2	0
1	5	.	5	0
2	1	.	0	5

Page 10:
a. Yes.
b.

Tens	Ones	Decimal Point	Tenths	Hundredths
2	0	.	5	0

Page 15:
a. Income
    $20.00
    $7.25
    $5.50
b. The total weekly income is $32.75.

Page 19:
a. Carlos has $12.00.
b. Carlos needs to save $10.50.

Page 22:
a. The DVD was $24.50.
b. Sam received $5.50 change:
    $30.00 − $24.50 = $5.50
    $5.50 − .75¢ = $4.75
    Sam has $4.75 left.

Page 25:
$3.50 + $3.50 = $7.00
Sam will earn $7.00 from doing Nisha's paper route for 2 days.

Problem-Solving Activity

50 hot dogs = $100.00. So 100 hot dogs:
$100.00 × 2 = $200.00
50 hot dog buns = $25.00. So 100 hot dog buns: $25.00 × 2 = $50.00
8 bottles of ketchup = $28.00
8 jars of mustard = $32.00

Expenses
        $200.00
        $50.00
        $28.00
        $32.00
Total: $310.00

a. Chris will earn $350.00
b. $350.00 income − $310.00 expenses = $40.00 profit
c. The club will be able to buy 8 uniforms.
   $40.00 profit ÷ $5.00 cost of uniform = 8 uniforms